MATHEMATICS
Practice
Questions

By Mark Patmore

Contents

The National Tests	3
How to use this book	4
Section 1: Level 4 Sample Test	6
Section 2: The Number System and Calculations	10
Section 3: Measures, Shape and Space	28
Section 4: Handling Data	38
Section 5: Level 5 Sample Test	50
Key Facts	58
Test tips and technique	60

The answers can be found in a pull-out section in the middle of this book.

Rising Stars UK Ltd., 76 Farnaby Road, Bromley, BR1 4BH

www.risingstars-uk.com

Every effort has been made to trace copyright holders and obtain their permission for the use of copyright material. The authors and publishers will gladly receive information enabling them to rectify any error or omission in subsequent editions.

All facts are correct at time of going to press.

This edition 2005

Text, design and layout © Rising Stars UK Ltd.

Editorial: Tanya Solomons
Design: Ken Vail Graphic Design, Cambridge
Layout: Branford Graphics
Cover design: Burville Riley
Illustrations: Burville Riley; Beehive Illustrations (Theresa Tibbetts); Graham-Cameron Illustration (Tony Maher) and Jim Eldridge

All rights reserved. No part of this publication may be reproduced, stored in a retrieval system, or transmitted in any form by any means, electronic, mechanical, photocopying, recording or otherwise without the prior permission of Rising Stars UK Ltd.

British Library Cataloguing in Publication Data

A CIP record for this book is available from the British Library.

ISBN 1-905056-07-9

Printed by Craft Print International Ltd, Singapore

The National Tests

Key Facts

★ The Key Stage 2 National Tests (or SATs) take place in the middle of May in Year 6. You will be tested on Maths, English and Science.

★ The tests take place in your school and will be marked by examiners – not your teacher!

★ You will get your results in July, two months after you take the tests.

★ Individual test scores are not made public but a school's combined scores are published in what are commonly known as league tables.

The Maths National Tests

You will take three tests in Maths:

- **Mental Maths Test** – This test will be played to you on a cassette. You will have to answer the questions mentally within 5, 10 or 15 seconds. This test will take about 20 minutes.

- **Test A** – The non-calculator test. This test requires quick answers on a test paper. You will not be able to use a calculator but should show any working you do.

- **Test B** – This test allows you to use a calculator and includes problems that will take you longer to solve.

Using and Applying Mathematics

There will be more questions than in previous years testing how you use and apply your mathematical knowledge in different situations. This includes knowing what is the important information in the questions, how to check your results, describing things mathematically using common symbols and diagrams, and explaining your reasons for conclusions that you make.

Much of the book is written to help you get into practice for these questions. It is also worth looking at these pages, which should help you with this area of Maths: pages 10–11, pages 34–35, pages 46–47 and pages 53–55.

You might be asked to explain your answers and write possible answers. Remember always to show your method.

How to use this book

Level 4 Sample Test (45 minutes)

① A warm-up test, which practises all the Level 4 Tricky Bits included in the Achieve Level 5 Maths revision book.

② Each question has space for the answers, a specific number of marks (like a real SATs question) and answers are included at the back of the book.

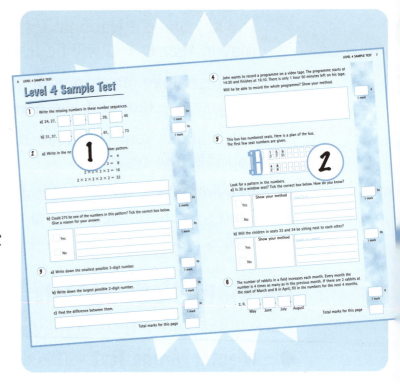

Topic questions

① A series of questions on all the topics you need to cover for the Maths Test, including some questions on Using and Applying Mathematics.

② Each topic matches a section in the Achieve Level 5 Maths revision book.

③ Each question has space for the answers, a specific number of marks (like a real SATs question) and answers are included at the back of the book.

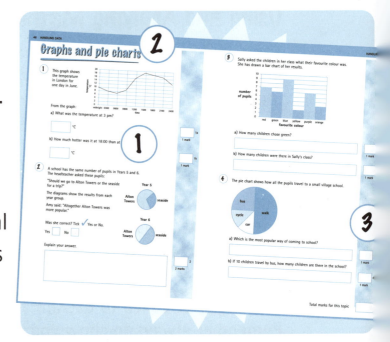

Level 5 Sample Test (1 hour)

1 A final test covering all the Level 5 content, which allows you to see which areas you have got to grips with and which areas you still need to revise. The Sample Test is similar to the real SATs, as it starts with some easy questions and gets harder as the test goes on.

2 Each question has space for the answers, a specific number of marks (like a real SATs question) and answers are included at the back of the book.

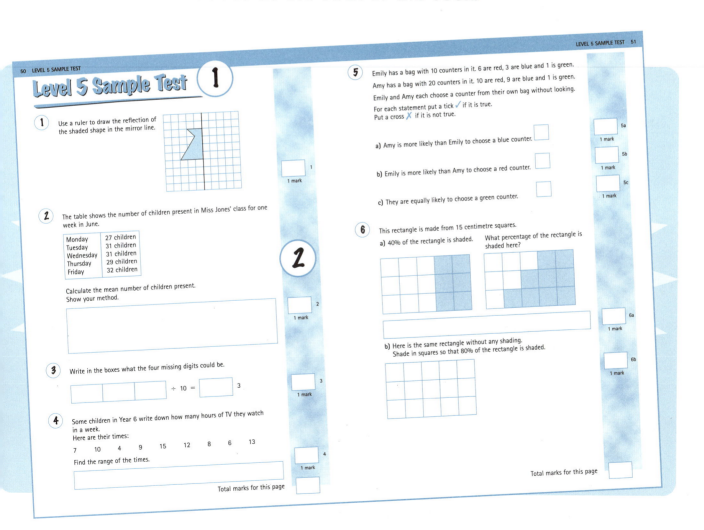

Level 4 Sample Test

1 Write the missing numbers in these number sequences.

a) 24, 27, ☐, ☐, ☐, 39, ☐, 45

1 mark

b) 31, 37, ☐, ☐, ☐, 61, ☐, 73

1 mark

2 a) Write in the next two rows in this number pattern.

$$2 \times 2 = 4$$
$$2 \times 2 \times 2 = 8$$
$$2 \times 2 \times 2 \times 2 = 16$$
$$2 \times 2 \times 2 \times 2 \times 2 = 32$$

2 marks

b) Could 275 be one of the numbers in this pattern? Tick the correct box below. Give a reason for your answer.

☐ Yes

☐ No

1 mark

3 a) Write down the smallest possible 3-digit number.

1 mark

b) Write down the largest possible 2-digit number.

1 mark

c) Find the difference between them.

1 mark

Total marks for this page

4 John wants to record a programme on a video tape. The programme starts at 14:30 and finishes at 16:10. There is only 1 hour 50 minutes left on his tape.

Will he be able to record the whole programme? Show your method.

5 This bus has numbered seats. Here is a plan of the bus.
The first few seat numbers are given.

Look for a pattern in the numbers.
a) Is 30 a window seat? Tick the correct box below. How do you know?

☐ Yes   Show your method   I know 30 is
☐ No

b) Will the children in seats 33 and 34 be sitting next to each other?

☐ Yes   Show your method   Explain your answer
☐ No

6 The number of rabbits in a field increases each month. Every month the number is 4 times as many as in the previous month. If there are 2 rabbits at the start of March and 8 in April, fill in the numbers for the next 4 months.

2, 8, ☐ , ☐ , ☐ , ☐
      May June July August

Total marks for this page

7 This diagram shows the number of flower beds in the local park. Some flower beds have only one colour of flower in them; some have more than one colour.

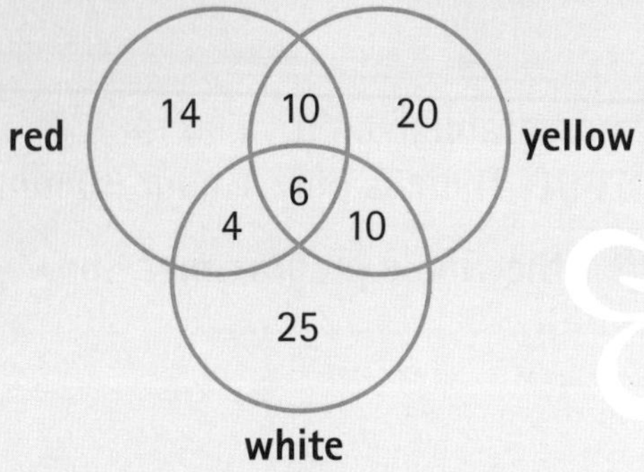

red: 14, 10, 20 :yellow
6
4, 10
25
white

a) How many flower beds have 3 colours of flower in them?

7a 1 mark

b) How many flower beds have only red and white flowers in them?

7b 1 mark

c) How many flower beds have yellow flowers in them?

7c 1 mark

8 Here are five number cards. 3 4 5 6 7

Use all five cards to make an addition sum that has the answer 430.

8 1 mark

9 Write down the missing numbers in sequence A and sequence B.

A	B
2	5
4	9
6	13
8	
	21

9 2 marks

Total marks for this page

Write down the relationship between the numbers in column B and the numbers in column A.
Show your method.

2 marks

10 401 children go to Holly Farm Junior School. The table shows how many classes there are in each year and how many children there are in each class.

	Number of classes in the year	Number of children in each class
Year 3	3	27
Year 4	3	28
Year 5	4	30
Year 6	4	29

Put numbers in the boxes so that the calculation gives the total number of children in the school.

(☐ × 27) + (3 × ☐) + (4 × 30) + (☐ × ☐) = 401

2 marks

11 This timetable shows the times of trains from Derby to London.

Derby	06:33	06:56	07:56	09:01
London	08:33	08:53	09:33	10:41

a) The train due to leave Derby at **07:56** actually left **7 minutes late**.

What time did it leave?

1 mark

b) The same train arrived in London 3 minutes early.

What time was that?

1 mark

c) How long did the journey take?

1 mark

Total marks for this page

Total marks for the test /25

Checking your answers

1 Write each of these numbers to the nearest whole number.

15.6 ☐   7²⁄₅ ☐   4.44 ☐

☐ 1
1 mark

2 Round the following numbers.

58 correct to the nearest 10 ☐

365 correct to the nearest 10 ☐

432 correct to the nearest 100 ☐

3299 correct to the nearest 1000 ☐

33 608 correct to the nearest 1000 ☐

☐ 2
1 mark

3 3400 + 726 = 4126
Amy checks the answer to this sum by calculating 4000 + 126.

Show how she would use the same method to check this sum.
2700 + 948

☐

☐ 3
1 mark

4 To check the answer to 532 × 7 you can use these methods:
532 × 7 = (532 × 10) − (532 × 3) or 532 × 7 = (500 × 7) + (32 × 7)

Fill in the boxes to check the answer to 496 × 8 in the same way.

496 × 8 = (☐ × 10) − (496 × ☐)

496 × 8 = (500 × ☐) − (☐ × ☐)

☐ 4
1 mark

5 The answer to 358 ÷ 4 lies between
360 ÷ 4 = 90 and 320 ÷ 4 = 80.

Show how you know the answer to 547 ÷ 8 lies between 60 and 70.
Show your method.

1 mark

6 Ross checks the answer to 3654 ÷ 42 = 87 by calculating 87 × 42 = 3654.

Ross wants to check that 14 376 ÷ 24 = 599.

Write down the calculation he could use to check his answer.

☐ × ☐ = ☐

1 mark

Total marks for this topic

Multiplying and dividing by 10, 100 and 1000

1 Put a ring round the correct answer.

210 ones is the same as:

21 hundreds   21 tens   210 tens   210 hundreds

1 mark

2 Put a ring round the number that is 100 times 140.

10 400   14 000   100 400   10 004 000

1 mark

3 Here is a number loop.

Write the missing numbers in the two boxes and the circle to make the loop complete.

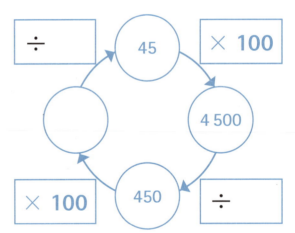

2 marks

4 Emily knows that 37 × 5 = 185

Show how she can use this information to find out the answer to this multiplication.

137 × 5

Show your method.

1 mark

5 Put numbers in the boxes to make these statements true.

190 × ☐ = 1900   546 ÷ ☐ = 5.46

☐ 5
1 mark

6 Circle two different numbers so that when the larger is divided by the smaller the answer is 100.

10   100   1000   10 000   100 000

☐ 6
1 mark

7 Strips of paper are each 25 cm long.

Amy joins strips of paper together to make a streamer for Christmas.

The strips overlap each other by 3 cm.

25 cm

3 cm

a) How long is a streamer made from only 2 strips?

Show your method.

☐ 7a
1 mark

b) Amy makes a streamer using 10 strips.

How long is the streamer?

Show your method.

☐ 7b
1 mark

Total marks for this topic ☐

Decimals

1 The arrow points to a number exactly halfway between 3 and 4.

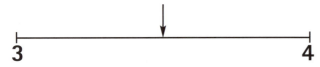

a) Write the number shown by the arrow as a decimal number. ☐   1a
    1 mark

This arrow points to a number exactly between 0.5 and 0.6.

b) Write the number shown by the arrow as a decimal number. ☐   1b
    1 mark

2 Circle the number closest in value to 0.5.

0.43   0.05   0.54   0.1   0.4

    2
    1 mark

3 Use a calculator to work out

5.46 × (3.14 + 2.86) = ☐

    3
    1 mark

4 Gel pens are 80p each.

Marker pens are £1.30 each.

Asif bought some gel pens and some marker pens. He spent £11.30.

How many of each type did he buy?

Show your method.

    4
    1 mark

5 Priya and Jodie are working on a number puzzle.

Find the two numbers that add up to 10 and multiply together to make 20.

Priya guesses 7.3 and 2.7

$\qquad$ 7.3 + 2.7 = 10 ✓

but $\quad$ 7.3 × 2.7 = 19.71 $\qquad$ too small

Jodie guesses 7.1 and 2.9

$\qquad$ 7.1 + 2.9 = 10 ✓

but $\quad$ 7.1 × 2.9 = 20.59 $\qquad$ too big

a) Make a better guess than either Priya or Jodie.

[ ] and [ ]

5a

1 mark

Use your calculator to check your guess.

b) [ ] + [ ] = [ ]

5b

1 mark

c) [ ] × [ ] = [ ]

5c

1 mark

Total marks for this topic [ ]

Reducing a fraction to its simplest form

1 Which is larger $\frac{2}{3}$ or $\frac{3}{5}$?

Show your method.

2 marks

2 Fill in the spaces in these equivalent fractions:

$$\frac{3}{5} \quad \frac{\square}{15} \quad \frac{30}{\square}$$

1 mark

3 Write the following fraction in its lowest terms: $\frac{12}{20}$

1 mark

4 Some of these fractions are the same as four-fifths, $\frac{4}{5}$.

Put a tick ✓ under those you think are the same.

Put a cross ✗ under those you think are not the same.

The first two have been done for you.

$\frac{16}{20}$ ✓ $\frac{12}{18}$ ✗ $\frac{8}{10}$ ☐ $\frac{20}{25}$ ☐ $\frac{24}{30}$ ☐ $\frac{12}{16}$ ☐

1 mark

5 Here is a pattern of shapes.

Underneath each shape write down the fraction of each shape that is shaded and simplify the fraction.

The first one has been done for you.

$$\frac{4}{6} = \frac{2}{3}$$

5 — 2 marks

6 Here is a shape.

What is the ratio of the shaded triangles to the unshaded triangles?

6 — 1 mark

7 Look at this pattern.

What is the ratio of shaded squares to white squares?

7 — 1 mark

Total marks for this topic

Calculating fractions or percentages

1) What fraction of this shape is shaded?

[1 mark]

2) At a wildlife park the butterfly house has a picture of a butterfly on the wall. On the picture the butterfly is 240 mm wide.
The width of the real butterfly is 25% of 240 mm.

a) How wide is the real butterfly? Show your method.

[2a, 2 marks]

Inside the butterfly house is a sign with a beetle on it.
On the sign the beetle is 100 mm long. The real beetle is $\frac{1}{4}$ of this length.

b) How long is the real beetle? Show your method.

[2b, 2 marks]

3) Flowers in a garden display are arranged in the following proportions:

Red	Yellow	Pink	Purple	White
10%	35%	20%	25%	10%

There are 200 flowers altogether.
Complete the table showing how many of each colour there are.

Red	Yellow	Pink	Purple	White

[3, 1 mark]

4 A larger packet of soap powder will hold 20% more than this packet.

How much will the larger packet hold?
Show your method.

750 g

2 marks

5 Amy asked 40 children in her school to name their favourite flavour of crisps.

flavour	number of children
plain	8
salt and vinegar	10
cheese and onion	4
barbeque	18

Which flavour did 20% of the children choose?
Show your method.

2 marks

6 The distance from A to B is one quarter of the distance from B to C.

The distance from B to C is 48 cm.

Calculate the distance from A to C.
Show your method.

A   B   C

48 cm

2 marks

Total marks for this topic

Multiplication and division

1 Write the correct digit in the box to make this multiplication correct.

23 ☐ × 8 = 1896

Show your method.

☐ 1

1 mark

2 Calculate 374 ÷ 22

Show your method.

☐ 2

1 mark

3 You can change the number 100 to the number 20 in different ways.
Write the missing numbers in the boxes.
The first one has been done for you.

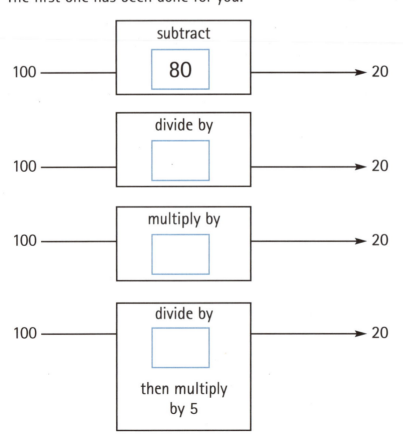

☐ 3a

1 mark

☐ 3b

1 mark

☐ 3c

1 mark

4 Here is a number loop:

Write the correct number in the box to make the loop complete.

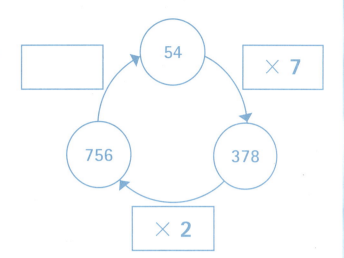

4
1 mark

5 Look at this number chain:

Fill in the missing numbers in the chains below.

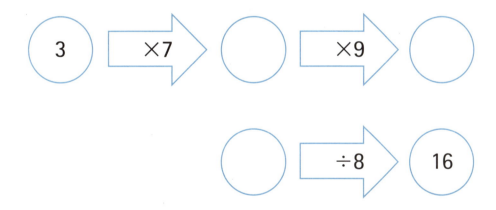

5a
1 mark

5b
1 mark

Total marks for this topic

Negative numbers

1) A sequence starts at 50 and 8 is subtracted each time.
a) Write the missing numbers in this number sequence.

50, 42, 34, ☐ , ☐

b) The sequence continues in the same way.
Write the first two numbers in the sequence that are less than zero.

☐ ☐

2) Here are some temperatures in different cities around the world for one day in December.

London 4°C   New York −3°C   Rome 8°C   Paris 2°C

a) Which was the coldest city?

b) Which was the warmest city?

c) What was the difference in temperature between them?
°C

3 Jodie and Tom are playing a game with plastic frogs on a number line. The aim is to move their frog to zero. They roll a dice and the score gives the number of jumps their frog can make.

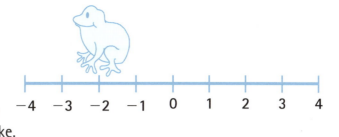

If the score is an even number, the frog jumps to the right. If the score is an odd number, the frog jumps to the left.

a) Jodie's frog is at −2.
   She rolls the dice and scores 4.
   What number does her frog jump to?

b) Tom's frog is at 3. He scores 5.
   What number does his frog jump to?

4 Look at this thermometer.
It measures temperature in degrees Celsius, °C

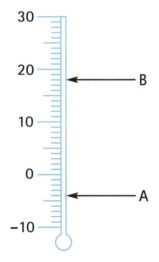

a) What temperature is shown by arrow A and by arrow B?

Arrow A ☐ °C   Arrow B ☐ °C

b) The temperature rose by 9 °C from that shown by arrow A.
   Write down the new temperature.

Total marks for this topic

Simple formulae

1 Fill in the empty boxes to complete the pattern.

n + 4	5n + 4	
	5n + 2	9n + 2
n		9n

2 marks

2 m and n each stand for whole numbers.

m + n = 500
m is 130 greater than n

Calculate the numbers m and n by trial and error.
Show your method.

m =   n =

2 marks

3 Here are some window sizes:

height in cm	10	15	20	25
length in cm	17	27	37	47

For each window the length is twice the height, subtract 3.

a) What is the length of a window that has a height of 40 cm?

cm

1 mark

For each window the length (L) is twice the height (H) subtract 3.

b) Write this in symbols.

L = [ ]

3b, 1 mark

c) A new window has its length three times its height.
It is made with 480 cm of wood.
What are the length and the height of this window?
Show your method.

[ ]

Length = [ ] cm   height = [ ] cm

3c, 2 marks

4 Here is a sequence of shapes made with matchsticks.

The sequence continues in the same way.
Calculate how many matchsticks there will be in shape 10.
Show your method.

[ ]

4, 2 marks

5 n stands for a number.
Match the equivalent expressions.
One has been done for you.

n times n		2n
5 subtract n		n²
n add 3		n + 3
		5 − n
		n − 5

5, 2 marks

Total marks for this topic [ ]

Using brackets

1 Fill in the missing numbers in the boxes.

(☐ × 9) ÷ 6 = 6

6 × (9 ÷ 3) = ☐

4² ÷ ☐ = 2

1 mark

2 Fill in the missing numbers in the boxes.

(3 + 2) × 5 = ☐

(☐ + 6) × 8 = 64

(19 × ☐) + 25 = 101

1 mark

3 a) Write down the answers to:

(4 + 2) × 3 = ☐   4 + (2 × 3) = ☐

1 mark

b) Work out the answer to: (3 + 4) × (4 + 5 + 1)
Show your method.

1 mark

c) Put brackets in this calculation to make the answer equal to 60.

5 + 6 + 1 × 5 = 60

1 mark

d) Put brackets in this calculation to make the answer equal to 40.

5 + 6 + 1 × 5 = 40

1 mark

4 Calculate: $\dfrac{36 \times 5 + (70 \times 2)}{20}$

Show your method.

5 Add brackets to make this statement true.

5 + 3 × 2 = 11

6 Put a number in the box to make this calculation correct.

(15 × 60) + ☐ = 1350

7 Work out: 78 × (79 + 24)

8 Work out:

a) 85 + (2 × 9) =

b) (85 + 2) × 9 =

9 Work out: $\dfrac{(34 \times 5) - (24 \times 4)}{2}$

Total marks for this topic

Coordinates

1 The shaded shape is a parallelogram.

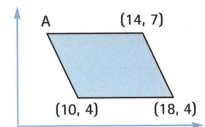

Write down the coordinates of point A.

1 mark

2 Here is a graph.

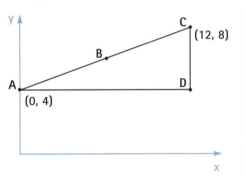

Point D is vertically below point C and directly across from point A.

What are the coordinates of point D?

(___ , ___)

The points A, B and C are equally spaced. What are the coordinates of point B?

(___ , ___)

2 marks

3 Look at the diagram:

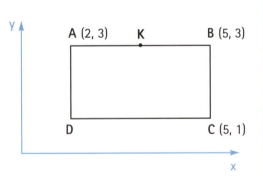

The point K is halfway between points A and B.
What are the coordinates of point K?

(___ , ___)

Shape ABCD is a rectangle.
What are the coordinates of point D?

(___ , ___)

2 marks

4 A straight line can be drawn through the crosses and circles on this grid.

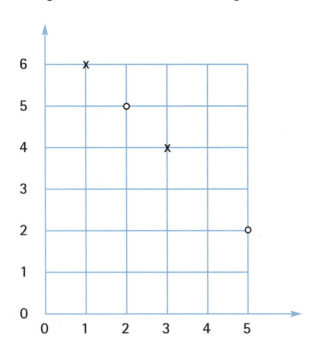

a) Put one more cross on the grid that is in the same straight line as the other crosses and circles.

4a
1 mark

b) Write the coordinates of the crosses and circles, in order.
The first two have been done for you.

(1, 6) (2, 5) (___, ___) (___, ___) (___, ___)

4b
1 mark

c) Look at the coordinates carefully to find any number patterns.
Write about two number patterns you have seen.

4c
1 mark

Total marks for this topic

Angles

1 Measure this angle:

A

a) Write your answer here [ ] °

1a 1 mark

b) Draw a line at an angle of 50° at A to make a triangle.

1b 1 mark

2 Look at the diagram:

Calculate the size of angle x and angle y.
Do not use a protractor.

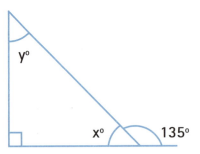

x = [ ] °

y = [ ] °

2 2 marks

3 Look at the diagram:

Calculate the size of angle x and angle y.
Do not use a protractor.

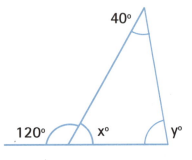

x = [ ] °

y = [ ] °

3 2 marks

MATHEMATICS
Answers for Practice Questions

Answers

Page 6

1. a) (24), (27), **30**, **33**, **36**, (39), **42**, (45)
   b) (31), (37), **43**, **49**, **55**, (61), **67**, (73)
2. a) $2 \times 2 \times 2 \times 2 \times 2 \times 2 = 64$
      $2 \times 2 \times 2 \times 2 \times 2 \times 2 \times 2 = 128$
   b) No – all answers are even numbers.
3. a) 100
   b) 99
   c) The correct answer should be 100 – 99 = 1 but accept 101 – 99 = 2 or 111 – 99 = 12
4. Yes. 14:30 to 16:10 is 1 hour 40 minutes.
5. a) Yes. Number sequence goes up in 4's.
      2, 6, 10, 14, 18, 22, 26, 30
   b) No. 34 is in one sequence of window seat numbers. 33 is in a different sequence of window seat numbers.
6. (2), (8), **32**, **128**, **512**, **2048**
7. a) 6   b) 4   c) 46
8. 354   or   376
    76   54
   430   430
9. 10   17   B = 2 times A + 1
10. ([3] × 27) + (3 × [28]) + (4 × 30) + ([4] × [29]) = 401
11. a) 08:03   b) 09:30   c) 1 hour 27 minutes

Page 10

1. 16, 7, 4
2. 60, 370, 400, 3000, 34 000
3. 3000 + 648
4. (496 × 10) – (496 × 2)   (500 × 8) – (4 × 8)
5. 560 ÷ 8 = 70   480 ÷ 8 = 60
6. 599 × 24 = 14 376

Page 12

1. 21 tens ringed
2. 14 000 ringed
3. (diagram: 45 → ×100 → 4500 → ÷10 → 450 → ×100 → 45 000 → ÷1000 → 45)
4. Recognition of 137 as 100 + 37 so that 137 × 5 = (100 × 5) + (37 × 5) = 500 + 185 = 685
5. 190 × 10 = 1900   546 ÷ 100 = 5.46
6. 1000 ÷ 10 or 10 000 ÷ 100 or 100 000 ÷ 1000
7. a) 47 cm   b) 223 cm [(10 × 25) – (9 × 3)]

Page 14

1. a) 3.5   b) 0.55
2. 0.54 circled
3. 32.76
4. 6 gel pens and 5 marker pens
5. Check the answers. Look for a number between 7.1 and 7.3 and 2.9 and 2.7
   Here are some possible answers:
   7.2 and 2.8 gives 20.16 – this is the expected answer
   7.21 and 2.79 gives 20.1159
   7.22 and 2.78 gives 20.0716
   7.23 and 2.77 gives 20.0271
   7.24 and 2.76 gives 19.9824

Page 16

1. $\frac{2}{3}$ identified as the larger fraction
   $\frac{2}{3} = \frac{10}{15}$ and $\frac{3}{5} = \frac{9}{15}$
2. $\frac{3}{5} = \frac{9}{15} = \frac{30}{50}$
3. $\frac{12}{20} = \frac{3}{5}$
4. $\frac{16}{20}$ ✓ $\frac{12}{18}$ ✗ $\frac{8}{10}$ ✓ $\frac{20}{25}$ ✓ $\frac{24}{30}$ ✓ $\frac{12}{16}$ ✗
5. $\frac{4}{6} = \frac{2}{3}$ $\frac{6}{12} = \frac{1}{2}$ $\frac{8}{20} = \frac{2}{5}$
6. 10 : 8 or 5 : 4
7. 10 : 10 or 1 : 1

Page 18

1. $\frac{3}{5}$
2. a) 60 mm   b) 25 mm
3. Total   200
   red   20
   yellow   70
   pink   40
   purple   50
   white   20
4. 20% of 750 = 150 g
   750 + 150 = 900 g
5. 20% of 40 = 8 therefore plain crisps
6. $\frac{1}{4}$ of 48 = 12
   therefore A to B = 12 cm
   therefore A to C = 60 cm

Page 20

1. 237 × 8
2. 17
3. a) 5   b) $\frac{1}{5}$ c) 25
4. ÷ 14
5. a) 3   ×7   21   ×9   189
   b) 128   ÷8   16

ANSWERS A3

Page 22

1. a) 26, 18 b) −6, −14
2. a) New York   b) Rome   c) 11 °C
3. a) 2   b) −2
4. a) A shows −4 °C; B shows 18 °C
   b) New temperature is 5 °C

Page 24

1. n + 4   5n + 4   9n + 4
   n + 2   5n + 2   9n + 2
   n   5n   9n
2. m = 315; n = 185
3. a) 77 cm   b) L = 2H − 3
   c) length = 180 cm   height = 60 cm
4. 33 matches
5. [n times n] linked to [n2]
   [5 subtract n] linked to [5 − n]
   [n add 3] linked to [n + 3]

Page 26

1. ([4] × 9) ÷ 6 = 6
   6 × (9 ÷ 3) = [18]
   4^2 ÷ [8] = 2
2. (3 + 2) × 5 = [25]
   ([2] + 6) × 8 = 64
   (19 × [4]) + 25 = 101
3. a) 18; 10
   b) 70
   c) (5 + 6 + 1) × 5 = 60
   d) 5 + ((6 + 1) × 5) = 40
4. 16
5. 5 + (3 × 2) = 11
6. 450
7. 8034
8. a) 85 + (2 × 9) = 103
   b) (85 + 2) × 9 = 783
9. 37

Page 28

1. (6, 7)
2. D is (12, 4)   B is (6, 6)
3. K is (3.5, 3)   D is (2, 1)
4. a) Cross drawn at (4, 3)
   b) (1, 6) (2, 5) (3, 4) (4, 3) (5, 2)
   c) Comments could include:
   x values increase by 1
   y values decrease by 1
   sum of the coordinates = 7

Page 30

1. a) 70° b) Line drawn at 50° at A to make a triangle.
2. x = 45°   y = 45°
3. x = 60°   y = 80°
4. x = 52°
5. x = 40°
6. x = 290°

Page 32

1.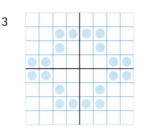
2. (grid diagram)
3. (coordinate grid diagram)
4. Flag B is facing the wrong way.   No
   The pencil on flag B is facing the wrong way.   Yes
   Flag B is too close to the mirror line.   Yes

Page 34

1. a) 124 000 g   b) 1.93 m
2. a) 3.75 kg   b) 750 g
3. a) divide by 1000
   b) multiply by 1000
   c) divide by 1000
4. 150 miles

Page 36

1. Check drawing. Possible answers are:
   3 × 8, 4 × 6
2. Total area: 7200 square centimetres
   Area of triangle: 1440 square centimetres
3. Largest number is 36 ÷ 4.5 = 8,
   65 ÷ 6.5 = 10, 8 × 10 = 80
4. Area of triangle = 21 cm^2
   Area of blue diamond = 84 cm^2
5. a) Area of large square = 20 × 20 = 400 cm^2
   b) Area of shaded square = 400 − (2 × (15 × 5)) = 250 cm^2

Page 38

1. 8
2. a) 10 = T ÷ 4 therefore T = 40
   b) Any 4 numbers whose total is 40, e.g. 18, 4, 6, 12
3. a) 5   b) 7
   c) e.g. the mean is the middle number
4. a) 28 birds   b) 7 birds
5. total = 140
   mean = 140 ÷ 10 = 14
6. total = 120
   mean = 120 ÷ 4 = 30

Page 40

1. 22
2. 13
3. 30
4. 6
5. 4
6. 9
7. 10

Page 42

1. a) Boys
   b) Boys
   c) Either boys because they had the largest mean or girls because their range was smaller.
2. 8
3. 8
4. 6
5. 6
6. 20
7. 2
8. 9
9. 10
10. 7

Page 44

1. 19
2. 13 cm
3. 31
4. 17
5. 5
6. 7
7. 6
8. 21

Page 46

1. a) 19 °C   b) 11 °C
2. Yes
   e.g. same number for each in Y6, more in Y5
3. a) 6   b) 33
4. a) walk   b) 40

Page 48

1. a) Arrow A at half
   b) Arrow B at one third
2. C
3. a) evens
   b) certain
   c) likely
   d) impossible
   e) unlikely
4. pupils in Y6   orange
   pupils in Y5   lemonade
   pupils in Y4   orange

Page 50

1.
2. total = 150
   mean = 150 ÷ 5 = 30
3. In the "hundreds" box any digit from 1 to 9 with the same digit in the "tens" box of the answer. 3 should be entered in the "tens" box.
   e.g. 5   3   0   ÷   10   =   5   3
4. 11 hours
5. a) Amy is more likely than Emily to choose a blue counter. ✓
   b) Emily is more likely than Amy to choose a red counter. ✓
   c) They are equally likely to choose a green counter. ✗
6. a) 60%
   b) Check – there should be 3 unshaded squares.
7. less than 1000   (736 − 427) ÷ 0.51
   more than 1000   89.5 + (94 × 9.9)
   equal to 1000   12.5 × (20.5 + 59.5)
8. (4, 3)
9. a) (180 × [2]) + ([140] × 1)
   b) £500
10. £14
11.

	300	40	6		
10	3000	400	60	---->	3460
6	1800	240	36	---->	2076
					5536

12. a) 999 × 15 = 14 985
       999 × 16 = 15 984
    b) 12 987 ÷ 999 = 13
       99 900 × 14 = 1 398 600
13. a) 17   b) 16
14. a) 63.1   b) 1.36   c) 36.1   d) 0.361
15. a) 38 cm   b) L = 2W + 2
16. a) toast   b) $\frac{1}{4}$ of 28 = 7
17. x = 60°   y = 50°
18. 2x = 200°   x = 100°
19. C   A   B
20. 1
21. £20.96
22. a) I am now 26 years old.   b) In 38 years' time, when I'm 64, my age will be both a square and a cube number.
23. 768
24. 35

Look at the diagram:

Calculate the size of angle x.
Do not use a protractor.

x = ☐ °

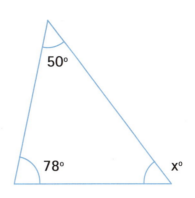

☐ 4

1 mark

Look at the diagram:

Calculate the size of angle x.
Do not use a protractor.

x = ☐ °

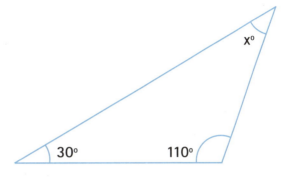

☐ 5

1 mark

Look at the diagram:

Calculate the size of angle x.

x = ☐ °

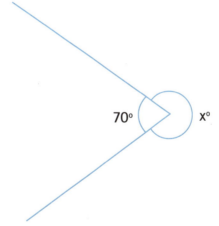

 6

1 mark

Total marks for this topic ☐

Symmetries of 2D shapes

1 Each of these shapes has one or more lines of symmetry.
Draw all the lines of symmetry on the shapes.

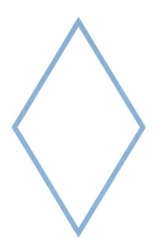

2 Draw the reflection of this shape in the mirror line.

3 Andrea is making a pattern using pegs and a peg board.
She wants the pattern to be symmetrical.

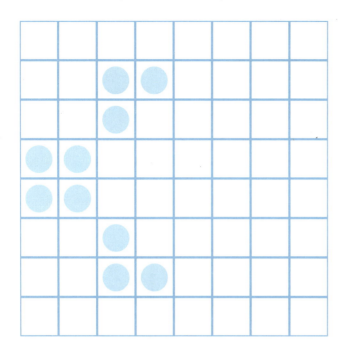

The pattern has two lines of symmetry.

Draw in both lines of symmetry.
The left side is already complete.
Complete the pattern to make it symmetrical.

4 Harry has drawn the reflection of flag A in the mirror line.
He labels the reflection B. His teacher asks him to look again.

Tick ✓ Yes or No for each of the following statements.

	Yes	No
Flag B is facing the wrong way.	☐	☐
The pencil on flag B is facing the wrong way.	☐	☐
Flag B is too close to the mirror line.	☐	☐

Total marks for this topic

Units of measure and estimating measures

1) Big Bill is 193 centimetres tall and weighs 124 kilograms.

a) Write his weight in grams.

[   ] g

1a
1 mark

b) Write his height in metres.

[   ] m

1b
1 mark

2)

1 kg 2 kg 3 kg 4 kg 5 kg

a) What is the total weight of these 5 balls?

[   ] kg

2a
1 mark

b) Each ball is the same weight.
How much does one ball weigh?
Write your answer in grams.

[   ] g

2b
1 mark

3 Complete the sentences to show how to change units.
The first one has been done for you.

To change litres to millilitres

| **multiply by 1000** |

a) To change millilitres into litres

| |

b) To change kilograms into grams

| |

c) To change grams into kilograms

| |

4 The distance from Ayton to Exton is 240 km.

5 miles is approximately 8 kilometres.

Use this fact to calculate the approximate distance in miles from Ayton to Exton.

Show your method.

Ayton
240 km
Exton

Total marks for this topic

The area of a rectangle

1 On the grid below, draw a rectangle with an area of 24 square centimetres.

1
1 mark

2 Here is a flag.

20% of the area of the flag is a triangle shaded grey.
What is the area of the shaded triangle?

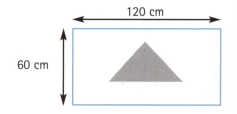

cm²

2
1 mark

3 Here are some tiles. Each tile measures 4.5 cm by 6.5 cm. Michelle uses the tiles to cover a table top which is a rectangle.

What is the largest number of tiles she needs?
Show your method.

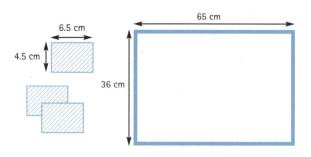

3
2 marks

4 A rectangular tile is divided into 2 halves, one grey and one white.

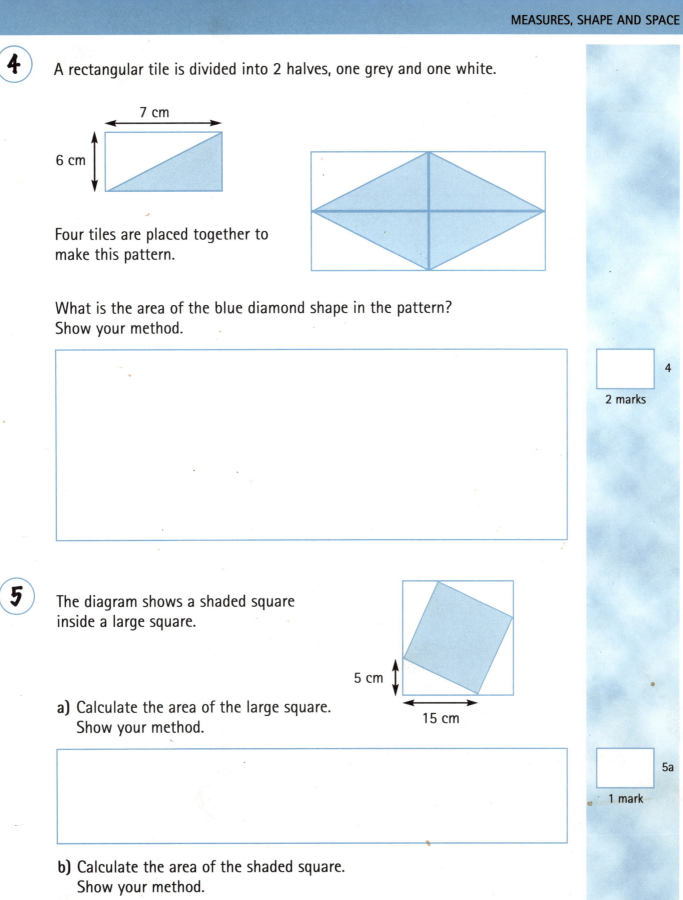

Four tiles are placed together to make this pattern.

What is the area of the blue diamond shape in the pattern?
Show your method.

4

2 marks

5 The diagram shows a shaded square inside a large square.

a) Calculate the area of the large square.
   Show your method.

5a

1 mark

b) Calculate the area of the shaded square.
   Show your method.

5b

1 mark

Total marks for this topic

Finding the mean

1) Find the mean of these four numbers: 4, 6, 10, 12
Show your method.

2) To calculate the mean of 4 numbers, Amy first adds them up and finds the total, T.
Then she divides the total, T, by 4. This gives her the mean.
The formula is mean $= T \div 4$
The mean of Amy's four numbers is 10.

a) What is the total of her 4 numbers?
Show your method.

b) What could the 4 numbers be?

3) **a)** Find the mean of 1, 3, 5, 7, 9
Show your method.

b) Find the mean of 3, 5, 7, 9, 11
Show your method.

c) Look at the numbers in a) and b). What do you notice about your answers?

4 John counts the number of birds at his bird table every hour during the morning.

| 9.00 | 10.00 | 11.00 | 12.00 |
| 10 birds | 6 birds | 8 birds | 4 birds |

a) How many birds came to his bird table?

b) Calculate the mean number of birds.
Show your method.

5 Karim measured the heights of 10 bean plants.
Here are his measurements:

12 cm   16 cm   13 cm   14 cm   18 cm
13 cm   15 cm   12 cm   13 cm   14 cm

Calculate the mean height.
Show your method.

6 The children in classes 3, 4, 5 and 6 collected tokens from crisp packets.
The table shows how many they collected on Monday.

Class 3	Class 4	Class 5	Class 6
24 tokens	36 tokens	20 tokens	40 tokens

What was the mean number of tokens collected on Monday?
Show your method.

Total marks for this topic

Finding the median

1 Here are the marks from a spelling test for the girls in class 6.

Jill	17
Emma	17
Charlotte	17
Wendy	21
Olivia	22
Sally	22
Gemma	23
Bridget	23
Safia	25
Bryony	25
Tanya	26

What is the median number of marks?

1 mark

2 Nadia measured the heights of 9 bean plants.
Here are her measurements:

12 cm   16 cm   13 cm   14 cm   18 cm
13 cm   15 cm   12 cm   13 cm

Find the median height.

1 mark

3 The table shows the number of children present in Miss Jones' class for one week in June.

Monday	29 children
Tuesday	31 children
Wednesday	31 children
Thursday	29 children
Friday	30 children

Calculate the median number of children present.

1 mark

4 Find the median of: 5, 10, 6, 8, 11, 5, 9, 1, 3

5 Find the median of: 1, 7, 5, 4, 7, 6, 2, 4, 3, 0, 5

6 Some children in Year 6 write down how many hours of TV they watch in a week.
Here are their times:

7 10 4 9 15 12 8 6 13

Find the median time.

7 Harry gives out the pots of pencils to each table in his class.
He counts the number of pencils in each pot.
Here are the numbers:

6 8 10 11 13

Find the median number of pencils.

Total marks for this topic

Finding the range

1 Miss Brown calculates the mean score and the range for pupils in a Year 6 maths test.
The table shows the means and ranges of the boys' and girls' scores.

	boys	girls
mean	24	21
range	10	3

a) Which group had the highest mean score?

b) Which group had the greatest range of scores?

c) Which group do you think did better? Explain your answer.

2 Find the range of these four numbers: 4, 6, 10, 12

3 Find the range of: 1, 3, 5, 7, 9

4 John counts the number of birds at his bird table every hour during the morning.

9.00   10.00   11.00   12.00
10 birds 6 birds 8 birds 4 birds

Find the range of the number of birds.

5 Karim measured the heights of 10 bean plants. Here are his measurements:

12 cm 16 cm 13 cm 14 cm 18 cm 13 cm 15 cm 12 cm 13 cm 14 cm

Find the range of the heights.

HANDLING DATA

6 The children in classes 3, 4, 5 and 6 collected tokens from crisp packets. The table shows how many they collected on Monday.

Class 3	Class 4	Class 5	Class 6
24 tokens	36 tokens	20 tokens	40 tokens

What was the range of the number of tokens collected on Monday?

1 mark

7 The table shows the number of children present in Miss Jones' class for one week in June.

Monday	29 children
Tuesday	31 children
Wednesday	31 children
Thursday	29 children
Friday	30 children

Calculate the range of the number of children present.

1 mark

8 Here are the marks from a spelling test for the girls in class 6.

Jill	17	Gemma	23
Emma	17	Bridget	23
Charlotte	17	Safia	25
Wendy	21	Bryony	25
Olivia	22	Tanya	26
Sally	22		

Find the range of the number of marks.

1 mark

9 Find the range for: 5, 10, 6, 8, 11, 5, 9, 1, 3

1 mark

10 Find the range for: 1, 7, 5, 4, 7, 6, 2, 4, 3, 0, 5

1 mark

Total marks for this topic

Finding the mode

1 Class 6 record the number of birds that visit the bird table each day between 10 am and 11 am for 2 weeks.
Here is the number of visits:

Monday	13	Monday	14
Tuesday	23	Tuesday	18
Wednesday	19	Wednesday	17
Thursday	19	Thursday	25
Friday	32	Friday	19

What is the mode of the number of visits?

1 mark

2 Karim measured the heights of 10 bean plants.
Here are his measurements:

| 12 cm | 16 cm | 13 cm | 14 cm | 18 cm |
| 13 cm | 15 cm | 12 cm | 13 cm | 14 cm |

Find the mode.

cm

1 mark

3 The table shows the number of children present in Miss Jones' class for one week in June.

Monday	27 children
Tuesday	31 children
Wednesday	31 children
Thursday	29 children
Friday	32 children

Find the mode.

1 mark

HANDLING DATA

4 Here are the marks from a spelling test for the girls in class 6.

Jill	17	Gemma	23
Emma	17	Bridget	23
Charlotte	17	Safia	25
Wendy	21	Bryony	25
Olivia	22	Tanya	26
Sally	22		

Calculate the mode.

1 mark

5 Find the mode of: 5, 10, 6, 8, 11, 5, 9, 1, 3

1 mark

6 Find the mode of: 1, 7, 5, 4, 7, 6, 2, 4, 3, 7, 5

1 mark

7 Some children in Year 6 write down how many hours of TV they watch in a week. Here are their times:

7   10   6   9   15   12   8   6   13

Find the mode.

1 mark

8 The temperatures in °C in Bournemouth for 2 weeks in June were:

24   24   23   21   18   17   19   21
21   21   25   24   22   26   20   18

Find the mode.

1 mark

Total marks for this topic

Graphs and pie charts

1 This graph shows the temperature in London for one day in June.

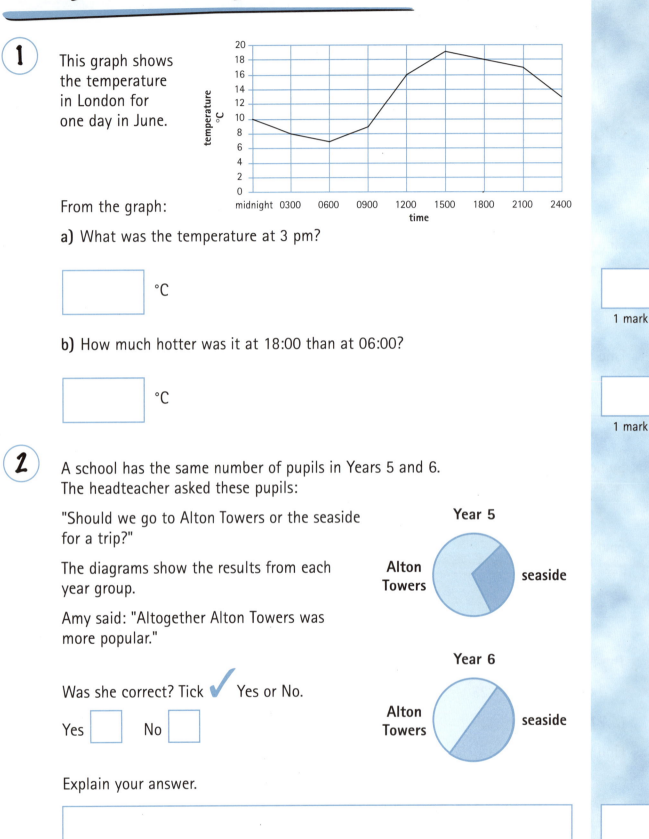

From the graph:

a) What was the temperature at 3 pm?

☐ °C

b) How much hotter was it at 18:00 than at 06:00?

☐ °C

2 A school has the same number of pupils in Years 5 and 6. The headteacher asked these pupils:

"Should we go to Alton Towers or the seaside for a trip?"

The diagrams show the results from each year group.

Amy said: "Altogether Alton Towers was more popular."

Was she correct? Tick ✓ Yes or No.

Yes ☐   No ☐

Explain your answer.

3 Sally asked the children in her class what their favourite colour was.
She has drawn a bar chart of her results.

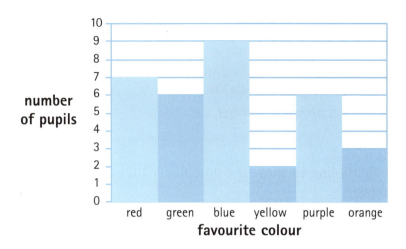

a) How many children chose green?

b) How many children were there in Sally's class?

4 The pie chart shows how all the pupils travel to a small village school.

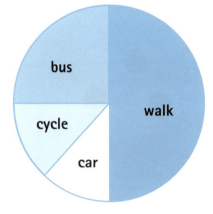

a) Which is the most popular way of coming to school?

b) If 10 children travel by bus, how many children are there in the school?

Total marks for this topic

The probability scale

1 A six-sided dice is rolled. Here are the facts:
- The probability that the dice will land on an odd number is a half.
- The probability that it will land on an even number is a half.
- The first time it is rolled it stops on an even number.

The dice is rolled again.

a) Draw an arrow on the probability line to show the probability that the dice will stop on an odd number.
Label this arrow A.

1 mark

0   ½   1

b) Draw another arrow on the probability line to show the probability that the dice will stop on a number in the 3 times table.
Label this arrow B.

1 mark

2 Each of these bags is shaken.
John takes a ball from each bag without looking.

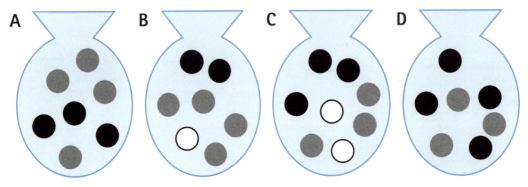

From which bag is the probability of taking a black ball the same as the probability of taking a grey ball?

1 mark

3 Here are 10 cards. Each card has a number on it.
The numbers are from 1 to 10.

The cards are placed face down.
Tim turns over a card.
Draw lines to show how likely it is that:

a) The card has an odd number on it.   likely

b) The card is more than 0.   unlikely

c) The card shows a number less than 10.   certain

d) The card shows the number 12.   impossible

e) The card shows a number in the 4 times table.   evens

3 marks

4 Some children in Years 4, 5 and 6 are asked about their favourite type of canned drink.

A pupil from each year group is chosen at random.

Do they prefer cola, orange or lemonade?

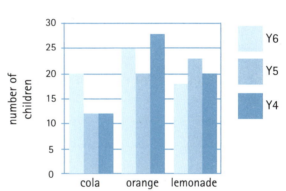

Tick ✓ the correct box in each row.

	cola	orange	lemonade
pupils in Y6	☐	☐	☐
pupils in Y5	☐	☐	☐
pupils in Y4	☐	☐	☐

3 marks

Total marks for this topic

Level 5 Sample Test

1 Use a ruler to draw the reflection of the shaded shape in the mirror line.

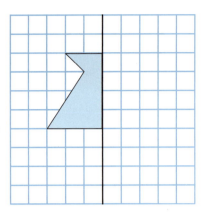

1 mark

2 The table shows the number of children present in Miss Jones' class for one week in June.

Monday	27 children
Tuesday	31 children
Wednesday	31 children
Thursday	29 children
Friday	32 children

Calculate the mean number of children present.
Show your method.

1 mark

3 Write in the boxes what the four missing digits could be.

☐ ☐ ☐ ÷ 10 = ☐ 3

1 mark

4 Some children in Year 6 write down how many hours of TV they watch in a week.
Here are their times:

7   10   4   9   15   12   8   6   13

Find the range of the times.

1 mark

Total marks for this page

5 Emily has a bag with 10 counters in it. 6 are red, 3 are blue and 1 is green.

Amy has a bag with 20 counters in it. 10 are red, 9 are blue and 1 is green.

Emily and Amy each choose a counter from their own bag without looking.

For each statement put a tick ✓ if it is true.
Put a cross ✗ if it is not true.

a) Amy is more likely than Emily to choose a blue counter. ☐

b) Emily is more likely than Amy to choose a red counter. ☐

c) They are equally likely to choose a green counter. ☐

6 This rectangle is made from 15 centimetre squares.

a) 40% of the rectangle is shaded. What percentage of the rectangle is shaded here?

b) Here is the same rectangle without any shading.
Shade in squares so that 80% of the rectangle is shaded.

Total marks for this page

7 Put a tick ✓ in the correct box for each calculation.

Use a calculator.
The first one has been done for you.

	less than 1000	equal to 1000	more than 1000
7.9 × 11.9 × 13.9			✓
(736 − 427) ÷ 0.51			
89.5 + (94 × 9.9)			
12.5 × (20.5 + 59.5)			

3 marks

8 Look at the grid.

ABCD is a square.

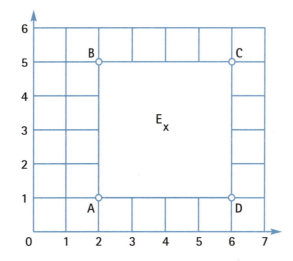

E is the centre of the square. What are the coordinates of point E?

1 mark

9 Tickets for the school pantomime cost £2 for adults and £1 for children.
180 adults and 140 children see the pantomime.

a) Fill in the boxes so that this calculation will give the amount of money received by the school.

(180 × £ ☐) + (☐ × £1)

1 mark

b) Work out how much money the school actually received.

1 mark

Total marks for this page

10 Five children collect money for a charity appeal.
Here is a bar chart of the amounts they have raised so far.

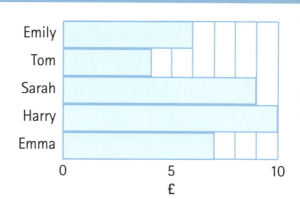

Their target is to collect £50.
How much more do they need to collect to reach the target?

10 1 mark

11 Nicola calculates the answer to 468 × 36 like this:

	400	60	8	
30	12 000	1 800	240	14 040
6	2 400	360	48	+ 2 808
				16 848

Use Nicola's method to calculate the answer to 346 × 16.

11 1 mark

12 Look at the way the digits change in this number pattern.
a) Use the pattern to fill in the missing numbers.

999 × 12 = 11 988
999 × 13 = 12 987
999 × 14 = 13 986

999 × ☐ = 14 985

999 × ☐ = ☐

12a 1 mark

b) Use the pattern to write down the answer to:

12 987 ÷ 999 = ☐   99 900 × 14 = ☐

12b 1 mark

Total marks for this page

13 At the school fayre Ben bought a bag with 10 packets of sweets in it.
He counted the number of sweets in each packet.
Here are his results:

15, 17, 14, 17, 16, 13, 17, 16, 18, 17

a) What is the mode of the number of sweets in a packet?

b) What is the mean number of sweets in a packet?

14 Emma has four cards.

One has a 6 written on it. One has a 3 written on it.
One has a 1 written on it. One has a decimal point . written on it.

a) What is the largest number she can make with all four cards?

b) What is the smallest number she can make with all four cards?

c) Emma puts the number 3.61 into her calculator.
She multiplies this number by 10.
What number should she see on the calculator display?

d) Emma puts the number 31.6 into her calculator.
She divides this number by 100.
What number should she see on the calculator display?

Total marks for this page

15 Here are some picture sizes.

width in cm	10	15	20	25
length in cm	22	32	42	52

width

length

For each picture the length is twice the width, add 2.

a) What is the length of a picture that has a width of 18 cm?

15a
1 mark

b) For each window the length (L) is twice the width (W), add 2.
Write this in symbols.

L =

15b
1 mark

16 This pie chart shows the favourite breakfast food of 28 pupils.

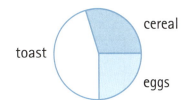

cereal

toast

eggs

a) Which was the favourite breakfast food?

16a
1 mark

b) How many pupils chose eggs?

16b
2 marks

17 Look at the diagram.

Calculate the sizes of angles x and y.
Do not use a protractor.

70°   y°   130°

x°

x = ⬜ °   y = ⬜ °

17
2 marks

Total marks for this page

18 Look at the diagram.

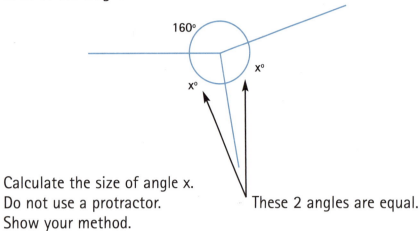

Calculate the size of angle x.
Do not use a protractor.
Show your method.

These 2 angles are equal.

2 marks

19 Look at the diagram.

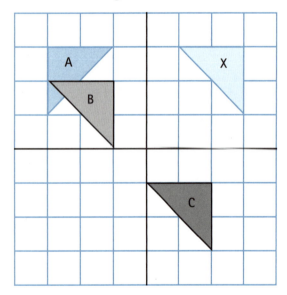

Fill in the boxes to make the statements true.

Triangle ☐ is a translation of triangle X, 1 square to the left and 4 squares down.

Triangle ☐ is a reflection of triangle X.

Triangle ☐ is a translation of triangle X, 4 squares to the left and 1 square down.

3 marks

Total marks for this page

20 This is a third: ○○

What is this? ○○○○○○ ☐

21 Six people pay £4.40 each for a meal in a restaurant. They leave a 10% tip for the waiter.
How much change do they receive from a £50 note?
Show your method.

22 Last year my age was a square number. Next year it will be a cube number.

a) How old am I?

b) How long must I wait until my age is both a square number and a cube number?

23 Each day the number of spiders under your bed doubles. On Monday, there were 6 spiders. How many spiders were there under your bed on the following Monday?

24 Martin has a video tape with three and a half hours of recording time. How many of his favourite 6 minute cartoons can he fit on the tape?

Total marks for this page

Total marks for the test ☐ / 50

KEY FACTS

The Number System and Calculations

Multiplying decimals by 10, 100 and 1000
- Shuffle numbers to the left.
- Shuffle numbers to the left once when × 10, twice when × 100 and three times when × 1000.

Dividing decimals by 10, 100 and 1000
- Shuffle numbers to the right.
- Shuffle numbers to the right once when ÷ by 10, twice when ÷ by 100, and three times when ÷ by 1000.

Negative numbers
- Integers are just whole numbers.
- When counting from negative up to positive or positive down to negative, **remember to count 0!**
- When counting on a number line, count to the right when adding, count to the left when subtracting.

Decimals to two places
- When rounding, remember 5 is up!
  6.785 = 6.79

Reducing a fraction to its simplest form
- If you are asked to find a proportion or ratio of two things or numbers you are being asked to find a fraction (in its lowest form).

Calculating a fraction or percentage
- Remember as many percentage/fraction equivalents as you can:

  $50\% = \frac{1}{2}$ $25\% = \frac{1}{4}$ $75\% = \frac{3}{4}$

  $33\% = $ nearly $\frac{1}{3}$ $66\% = $ nearly $\frac{2}{3}$

Multiplication and division (with decimal points)
- × and ÷ are opposites.
- Always estimate first. It will help you to get the decimal point in the right place if one is needed.

Checking your answers
- Inverse means opposite!
- Check addition by subtraction – and vice versa.
- Check division by multiplication – and vice versa.
- Use 'friendly numbers' when estimating: 2, 5, 10 etc.

Simple formulae
- **Talk** through the formula in your head. It will make it easier.

Brackets
- Always do brackets in equations first.

Coordinates
- Always read ALONG (x axis) and then UP (y axis).
- Always write (x) before (y) – (x, y).
- Quadrants work **anti-clockwise**.

3 o'clock to 12 o'clock = Quadrant 1
12 o'clock to 9 o'clock = Quadrant 2
9 o'clock to 6 o'clock   = Quadrant 3
6 o'clock to 3 o'clock   = Quadrant 4

Measures, Shape and Space

2D shapes
- Pentagon
  Pentagons have FIVE sides.
  Regular pentagons have FIVE EQUAL SIDES.
- Parallelogram
  A parallelogram is a RECTANGLE THAT HAS BEEN PUSHED OVER.
  Remember the opposite sides are the same length but parallel.
- Isosceles and scalene triangles
  An isosceles triangle has TWO EQUAL SIDES AND TWO EQUAL ANGLES.
  Picture an isosceles triangle as an arrow!
  A scalene triangle has THREE SIDES OF DIFFERENT LENGTHS and THREE ANGLES OF DIFFERENT sizes.
  When picturing a scalene triangle, think of SCALING A MOUNTAIN that has an easy way up or a more difficult side to climb!

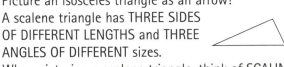

Angles
- Acute angle = 0–89°
- Right angle = 90°
- Obtuse angle = 91–179°
- Straight line = 180°
- Reflex angle = 181–359°
- Angles around a POINT always add up to 360° (a complete turn).
- The angles of a TRIANGLE always add up to 180°.

Symmetries
- When drawing reflections, remember to keep the correct distance from the mirror line.

Metric and imperial conversions (approximate)
- 1 litre = 1.8 pints
- 1 kilogram = 2.2 lbs (pounds)
- 1 pound = 0.454 kg
- 1 mile = 1.6 km
- 5 miles = 8 km
- 1 foot = 30 cm
- 1 metre = 3 feet 3 inches
- 1 inch = 2.5 cm

Estimating measures
- Milli = very small
- Centi = small
- Kilo = big

Area of a rectangle
- Area of a rectangle = length (L) × width (W)
- Area is always units squared (cm^2, m^2, mm^2)

Handling Data

Pictograms
- With pictograms PICTURE = NUMBER
  e.g. 🍦 = 20 ice creams 🍦 = 10 ice creams

Mean, median, range, mode
- Mean = sum of all numbers divided by number of numbers
- Median = middle number in sequence (always write down in order first)
- Range = difference between highest and lowest number
- Mode = most common value

Charts and graphs
- Be careful and accurate. Use a sharp pencil.
- Pie charts are good for percentages, fractions or decimals.

Probability scale
- Always goes from 0 to 1 (you need fractions/decimals here).

Test tips and technique

Before the test

1. When you revise, try revising a 'little and often' rather than in long sessions.
2. Learn your multiplication facts up to 10×10 so that you can recall them instantly.
3. Revise with a friend. You can encourage and learn from each other.
4. Get a good night's sleep the night before.
5. Make sure you have breakfast!
6. Bring your own pens and pencils and wear a watch to check the time.

During the test

1. Don't rush the first few questions. These tend to be quite straightforward, so don't make any silly mistakes.
2. As you know by now, READ THE QUESTION THEN READ IT AGAIN.
3. If you get stuck, don't linger on the same question! You can come back!
4. Never leave a multiple choice question. Guess if you really can't work out the answer.
5. Check how many marks a question wins. Will your answer earn each mark?
6. Check each answer, perhaps using the inverse or rounding method.
7. Be aware of the time. After 20 minutes, check to see how far you have got.
8. Try to leave a couple of minutes at the end to read through what you have written.
9. Show your method as this may win a mark even if your answer is wrong.
10. Don't leave any questions unanswered. In the two minutes you have left yourself at the end, make an educated guess at the questions you really couldn't do.

Things to remember

1. If you see a difficult question, take your time, re-read it and have a go!
2. Check every question and every page to be sure you don't miss any!
3. If a question is about measuring, always write in the UNIT of MEASUREMENT.
4. Don't be afraid to ask a teacher for anything you need, such as tracing paper or a protractor.
5. Write neatly – if you want to change an answer, put a line through it and write beside the answer box.
6. Always double-check your answers.